THE WANDERER IN AFRICA

An Enlightening Tale Illustrating The Thirty-Second Psalm

GREAT CHRISTIAN BOOKS
LINDENHURST, NEW YORK

THE
WANDERER
IN AFRICA

An Enlightening Tale Illustrating
The Thirty-Second Psalm

A. L. O. E.
the pseudonym of
Charlotte Maria Tucker

A GREAT CHRISTIAN BOOKS publication
Great Christian Books is an imprint of Rotolo Media
160 37th Street Lindenhurst, New York 11757
(631) 956-0998
www.GreatChristianBooks.com
email: mail@greatchristianbooks.com
The Wanderer in Africa

ISBN 978-1-61010-100-4 Paperback

Tucker, Charlotte Maria, 1821–1893 (a.k.a. A.L.O.E.)
The Wanderer in Africa / by A. L. O. E.
p. cm.
A "A Great Christian Book" book
GREAT CHRISTIAN BOOKS an imprint of Rotolo Media
ISBN 978-1-61010-100-4
Recommended Dewey Decimal Classification: 234
Suggested Subject Headings:
1. Religion—Christian literature—The Christian Life
2. Christianity—The Bible—Christian Living
I. Title

The book and cover design for this title are by Michael Rotolo
(www.michaelrotolo.com). It is typeset in the Minion typeface by
Adobe Inc. and is quality manufactured in the great United States
on premium, archival quality acid-free paper stock. To discuss the
publication of your Christian manuscript or out-of-print book,
please contact Great Christian Books. www.greatchristianbooks.com

MANUFACTURED IN THE UNITED STATES OF AMERICA

CONTENTS

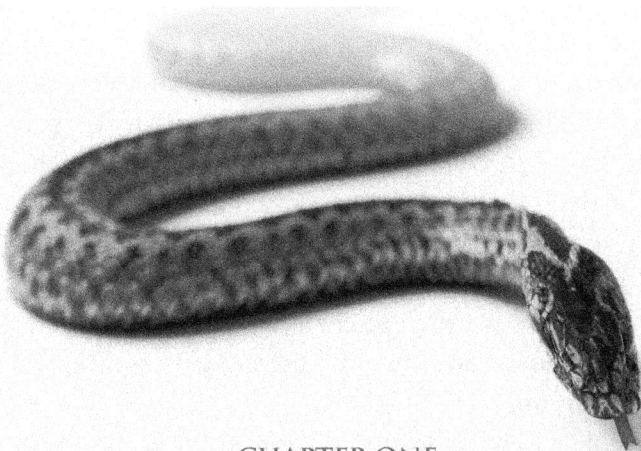

CHAPTER ONE

NIGHT ON THE WASTE

"Blessed is he whose transgression is forgiven, whose sin is covered. Blessed is the man unto whom the Lord imputeth not iniquity, and in whose spirit there is no guile." —Psalm 32: 1, 2

"No use, it won't do; rhinoceros hide won't get another yard out of them beasts! We must unyoke the oxen for the night!" exclaimed Hans Kuhe, the Dutch *Boer* (farmer at the Gaps colony), after Pollux, his Hottentot driver, had been for an hour belaboring, with the huge whip, eight unfortunate oxen that were vainly trying to drag his wagon through a sandy African waste.

"If we could but have reached water;—the poor beasts are dying of thirst," observed David, an English lad who was servant to the Boer. "Eight oxen are not enough to draw that heavy wagon."

And he looked with pity at the panting creatures, whose sides were seamed with weals, and bleeding from the whip which Pollux had plied with such merciless force. Hans muttered a curse on the four oxen that had died on the road, and a fiercer one upon the Bushmen who had carried off two others during the night. He was a large, bulky man, with coarse features bloated by intemperance; his brandy bottle and his pipe being his two constant companions.

"Help Pollux to unyoke 'em. Don't stand there like a lazy cur, as you are!" exclaimed the Boer to the English lad, who had done nine-tenths of all the work since the expedition had started. "No sulky looks for me,—and why do you go limping like that?" The question was asked in a tone of anger, by no means that of pity.

"That fore ox kicked me on the ankle," said David.

"You're an awkward cub!" growled the Boer. "No time to be lame now—you've got a thirty-miles walk afore ye tomorrow, 'fore we get to the Quagga Fountain. Now make haste, will ye, and take the yoke off that beast."

"Who will take the yoke off *me*?" thought the poor lad, as, biting his lip to repress either anger or pain, he proceeded to help to outspan the oxen for the night.

But a year before, David Aspinall had been a fine specimen of an English youth, with strength in his well-knit limbs, and careless mirth in his eyes, and a light heart in his bosom, which knew little of sorrow or care. *Now*, the sun-burnt cheek had grown hollow, and the eye had lost all its brightness, and the clothes hung loosely on the wasted limbs, and the expression of his face told of hard ship and grief, borne silently, but felt none the less.

"It has been my own choice, this path of misery; it has been my own putting on, this intolerable yoke of bondage!" so thought David, as he went on with his occupation. "The wages of sin—the wages of sin—ay, I know what they come to! I have none to blame but myself! I might have been "—but as that *might have been* was too bitter a reflection to dwell on, David tried to drive it away.

The evening's work was done. Hans, after a heavy meal of beltong (a beef jerky) taken with a large amount of brandy, sat on the wagon shaft, smoking his pipe in lazy enjoyment, and his weary, almost worn-out servant was suffered to take his food. There was nothing that would have refreshed David so much as to have plunged his aching head into cold water, and so have quenched his feverish thirst; but the small supply left in the water-jar was precious, and he scarcely received enough to relieve his most pressing need.

"Now I'm going to turn in," said Hans Kuhe, who, after the fashion of African travellers, made a house of his wagon; "Davy—you must keep watch tonight, for Pollux is not to be trusted; there he lies snoring already! We may have some of the Bushmen thieves down on us again, or the hyenas may come slinking to see what they can carry off, or a lion may get scent of the cattle. I fancy I heard a roar in the distance. You keep the double-barreled gun beside you, and mind, no sleeping on watch, or I'll give you a taste of the rhinoceros hide!"

The bulky form of the Boer soon disappeared, under the tilt of the wagon. David Aspinall was left to watch through the long weary hours in the dreary African waste. Night was there, but without its stillness. The painful lowing of the thirsty oxen, the occasional loud barking of the dogs whom a sense of danger seemed to keep wakeful, the howling of jackals, and the wild laugh of the hyenas in the distance, made together a horrible concert, which combined with the pain in his ankle to keep the weary lad from sleeping.

Would you wish to know the thoughts that passed through his mind, as resting on the sands, with his back against one of the huge wheels of the heavy wagon, and the double-barreled gun close to his hand, David sat with his eyes fixed on the large round moon which seemed to hang so near to earth, and which threw such black shadows of every object on the waste?

"A blessing and a curse were set before me; I left the blessing, and chose the curse! I was taught the right way, I was told my duty, I had parents who tried to lead me heavenwards, both by their words and their example. I had a conscience, but I would not listen to it; a Bible, but I cared not to read it. What would I not give for that Bible now! I have not set eyes on one for months! I wonder if I could remember anything of what I learnt by heart when I was a child at Greenside Farm!" and David began half aloud: " '*The Lord is my Shepherd, I shall not want. He maketh me to lie down in green pastures; He leadeth me beside the still waters.*' I can't go on with that," murmured the poor lad with a choking sensation at his throat, as his memory recalled soft green meadows, spangled with buttercups and daisies, in which he had romped when a child, and the little gurgling stream sparkling in the sunshine, as it flowed from under the shadow of the one arched bridge.

"That Psalm is not for me, not for a wandering sheep; it is for God's own flock, who hear His voice, and follow Him. I'm afraid I can remember no other: yes, there's the thirty-second Psalm, my mother's favorite, perhaps I could get through that. "*Blessed is he whose transgression is forgiven, whose sin is covered. Blessed is the man unto whom the Lord imputeth not iniquity, and in whose spirit there is no guile!*' " David stopped short, and pressed his feverish brow. "That Psalm may be for me, for it is for the wanderer; it speaks of transgression and sin,—and Oh!—it speaks of forgiveness and blessing! Can it be that I, wretched, desolate as I am, can be blessed?"

David looked earnestly up at the bright clear moon, as if to read an answer to his question there. She could smile in the desert, even as she had smiled on the meadows, and the trees, and the flowing stream by his English home; nay, she looked larger and lovelier here, as the air was clearer. "Blessed—blessed," repeated David to himself, as if he had difficulty in taking in the meaning of the words. "But *how* can transgression be forgiven, and *how* can sin be covered?"

Then in that wild solitude there came back on the memory of the poor lad lessons learned on the knee of his mother, lessons which had seemed till that moment forgotten; sermons heard in the quiet little church on the hill, whither he had often gone so unwillingly, where he had listened so carelessly to the message of "good tidings" from the lips of his pastor. David was not ignorant of the truths of the Gospel, but it had seemed as if, with him, the good seed had fallen by the wayside, and that pride, selfishness, and folly, like the birds of the air, had carried it all away. But it was not really so; some had rested on his memory, and now in the dreary African land were to spring up and bear good fruit. Very familiar to the ear of David Aspinall had been the verse, "*The blood of Jesus Christ His Son cleanseth from all sin;*" but he had never cared in his days of selfish mirth to apply its meaning to himself. David then had taken his sins too little to heart to reflect whether his could ever be cleansed away. He had welcomed Christmas year after year, but merely as a time of mirth and feasting; it had seemed little to him that a Savior had deigned to be born into the world which He had made,—for David had felt no need of a Savior.

It was different now: all the lad's earthly hopes had been crushed, all his earthly happiness had vanished away. David had offended against the laws of his country; he had found no mercy from man, and he feared the just anger of God. David had nothing left to cling to but the hope of forgiveness, and he knew, he had been taught from his childhood, that forgiveness, though freely offered to all, could only be procured by *any* through faith in a crucified Savior, *who died,—the Just for the unjust!*

It was long since David had prayed; perhaps it might more truly be said that he had never prayed in his life, for what are words without thoughts, the service of the lips without the love of the heart? David's first real prayer for forgiveness arose as he sat by the wheel of that great wagon, with the yells of wild beasts sounding in his ears. In his spirit there was at least *no guile*. He did not deceive himself as to his state before God; he made no excuses for his errors; he felt from the bottom of his heart that he was a sinner, and deserved all the misery that he endured. He knew that it would be a mockery of God to ask pardon for *the past*, without also asking for grace for *the future*, to lead a new and better life. David was honest in his repentance; sincere in his sorrow for sin. Alas! there are too many who mistake the mere cry of distress, under sharp affliction, for the penitent grief of a broken and contrite heart!

David had unconsciously clasped his hands in prayer; when he had unclasped them, he accidentally put his left hand down towards the ground, and was startled as it touched something clammy, which moved under his touch as if alive. The next moment the full moonlight fell on a large black poisonous snake, rapidly gliding away over the sand! It had been coiled up quite close to the lad, so close as to have been concealed by his own shadow! There had David rested in perfect ignorance of the deadly enemy so near, that an incautious movement on his part, by hurting and irritating the reptile, might have cost him his life!

David made no attempt to pursue the serpent; his foot had by this time swelled so much that he could hardly have put it to the ground, and to have broken the heavy sleep of Hans for so commonplace an event in the African desert as the appearance of a poisonous snake, would only have drawn upon himself the savage anger of the Boer.

But the visit of the reptile had not been without its effect on the mind of David, occurring as it had done at an hour of penitence and prayer. He felt that a pitying Providence had been watching over him, and a hope arose that he had been spared for future good, that his painful life had not been lengthened except for some purpose of mercy and love. As David silently returned thanks to God for having saved him from the fangs of the serpent, he almost felt as if this deliverance were a pledge that his prayer had been heard, and that his sins were forgiven. Oh! if he could but be at peace with God, then indeed might he face all his miseries with a firm and undaunted soul!

The next moment the full moonlight fell on a large black poisonous snake, rapidly gliding away over the sand!

Then followed other thoughts, suggested by the wild howls of the jackals and hyenas, smelling the scent of food, yet not daring to attack the travelling party. "Those sounds used to frighten me when I was new to them," thought David, "and even now they sent a thrill through me which was something like fear. I listened to them, and looked to my musket, and kept watchful and ready; but I was utterly careless of the far greater danger close by, the venomous serpent coiling so near! It is like what happens to us in life. We are watchful against external dangers,—we try to guard against poverty, sickness and pain, and yet we let the venomed serpent of sin lie in our bosom, though we know that its bite is death!"

David remained wakeful at his post, till the approach of the dawn made the wild creatures of the desert retire. Then indeed his thoughts became very dim and confused; a sound as of church bells was in his ears, like the invitation to come and worship which he had so often heard in the country of his birth, and so often of late months refused to accept. Then he was no longer in the dry and thirsty waste, the heavy wagon with its great canvas tilt, the broad wheels—the tired oxen resting around,—all had disappeared from his view. David dreamed that he was in the little church on the hill, sitting by the side of his mother in the well-remembered seat close to the pillar. He had often sat there when he was a boy, impatient for the end of the service, with thoughts intent on the thrush's nest that he had seen in the thicket, or the jackdaw's brood that he hoped to bring down from the old ruined tower. David had grudged the time spent in church; and now that church in his dream appeared to him almost like heaven! There was the well-known hymn—"Rock of Ages, cleft for me!"—swelling in the slumberer's ear, and David could distinguish the tones of his mother's voice, but sweeter than they ever had sounded before!—and then he seemed to be listening to the aged white headed pastor, whose sermons he once had thought so long,—and the silver hair above his brow looked to the dreaming youth like a glory! He was preaching about the Prodigal Son, and the joy in the father's home—and the father's heart—when the lost one again was found! David fancied that he caught the sound of his mother's sob, and that the old clergyman's eyes were fixed on him, and that he knew that he *himself* was the prodigal welcomed back,—never to wander again! The last words that rang in David's ear before his sweet dream was rudely broken, were the words of the Psalm that his mother loved,—the words that had brought to him comfort and hope, "*Blessed is he whose transgression is forgiven, and whose sin is covered.*"

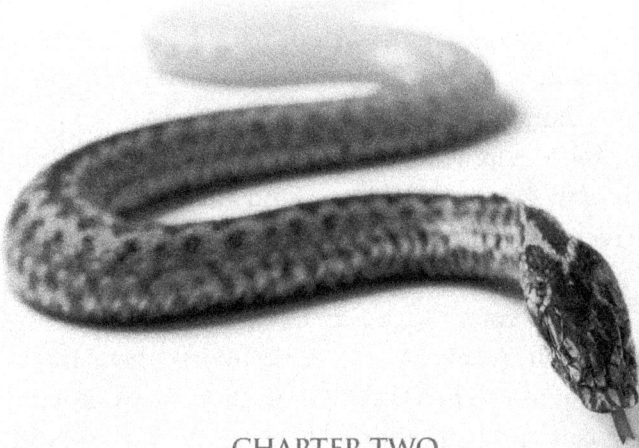

CHAPTER TWO

WANDERINGS

"When I kept silence, my bones waxed old, through my roaring all the day long. For day and night Thy hand was heavy upon me; my moisture is turned into the drought of summer." —Psalm 32: 3, 4.

While the exhausted lad is sleeping on his hard couch of sand, I will briefly relate the story of his past life, and tell the circumstances which led to his being a *Wanderer in Africa*, and in the service of Hans Kuhe, the Boer.

David Aspinall was the son of a small farmer in Dorsetshire,—an honest, God-fearing man, who had held a blameless course through life, looking to the Life beyond the tomb. He had no other son than David, but he had five little daughters, all of whom were younger than their brother. With so many mouths to feed, the farmer had little to spare, though many a poor neighbor had a slice of bacon, or a jug of skimmed milk from his good wife's dairy.

John Aspinall's strong wish was to bring up this only boy as his helper, and then successor at Grreenside Farm. He felt that his own health was frail, and his life even more uncertain than that of most other men. "It's a comfort to me," he would say to himself, when he was more poorly than usual, "that there will be Davy to look after the place, and take care of his mother and sisters, if so be as God should please to take me."

But David's plans for himself were very different from those of his father for him. He wanted to see life, to go into the world, to have something more exciting to do than foddering cattle, or shearing sheep, or driving the plough a-field. David was a sharp, clever lad, sure to make his way to fortune, at least his vanity told him so, and not the boy to be buried in a small out-of-the-way farm!

The time came when a decision must be made. After a sharp attack of rheumatic fever, which had made him feel more than ever that he needed the help of his son, John Aspinall, one day late in April, explained his wishes and those of his wife to David. The lad was somewhat taken aback. He had that very morning been poring over the advertisements in a newspaper, and calculating how much money it would take to carry him up to London, and thinking what grand things he might do and what a great man he might become, if he could once "get a fair start in life." David had always been a wild and willful boy, ready for any sport or fun, and the idea of being shut up all his life at Greenside Farm was more than his spirit would bear.

Here now were two paths open before David Aspinall; the way of duty,—*God's way*, and his own way,—the path of *Self-will*. The lad was not long in choosing between them. He said, indeed, how much he should like to please his father, only he could not please him in *this*. He kissed his mother fondly, but he grieved her none the less. He made little presents to all his sisters, and promised them fine things from London, but he would not give up for their sakes that upon which he had set his own heart.

John Aspinall was not a man of words: his face sharpened by pain, and the crutch which he used, said more than he could say; he let his son know his wishes, and then suffered him to follow his own. "We can't make the lad bide here against his will," observed the farmer to his wife: "it may please God to give me back health,—and if not, He'll care for you and our poor little lasses." The mother turned aside to dry her tearful eyes, and hoped and prayed that all might turn out for the best. It was a sore disappointment not to be able to keep Davy at home— but she would send him to her own worthy brother, the grocer in London; he could learn nothing but good with him, and would be kept out of the way of temptation.

So two of the pigs were sold to pay expenses, and David, in high glee, prepared to bid farewell to the little farm in the valley, and the sad and loving hearts that he would leave behind him. It touched him a little, indeed, to see how pale his mother's cheek had grown, and how red and tearful were the eyes of poor Jenny, the eldest but one of his sisters, as she sat stitching at his new shirts. She had been his especial playmate and pet, and loved him more than she loved anyone else upon earth.

"Well, Jenny, don't look so down-hearted!" cried the lad, as he came and seated himself by her side; "I can't bear to see you so doleful."

"And I can't bear to see you so merry just when you're going to leave us all," answered the girl, with a broken voice.

"I'm not so merry now, Jenny; I can't help having a bit of a twinge when I think of saying Good-bye."

"Then why should you say it?" exclaimed Jenny, dropping her work in her eagerness to speak."

"Oh Davy, Davy! stay with us—we cannot get on without you,—the farm will seem so lonely—so dreary! Even little Nelly will miss you so,—there will be no brother to dance her on his knee, or whistle her favorite songs! I shall never care to see the green leaves budding again, nor to hear the cuckoo, for they will always remind me of the time when Davy went to London! Oh! don't go,—stay with us, Davy! why should we not all be happy together?" and the poor girl burst into tears.

Davy kissed away the tears, and patted his sister on the shoulder, and said that he would be always thinking of her, that he would often write home, and maybe would come to old Greenside Farm at Christmas,—and would not they have rare fun then! David felt the appeal to his affections: he loved his parents, and his little sisters, and the dear old home; but he loved *himself* best of all. Therefore he resolved to go up to London.

Another effort was made to keep the willful lad at his home. Minnie, the eldest of the girls, gentle, thoughtful, and good, her father's comfort, her mother's right hand, felt that it would be right to try one more appeal to her brother's sense of duty. As Davy was on his knees, on the evening before the day fixed on for his departure, beginning to pack his box, he heard her gentle tap at the door.

"Come in," said Davy, looking up. "So, Minnie, you've come to help me, like a dear good child as you are!"

"Not exactly that," said his sister, "though I should be glad to help you to pack if—if you indeed must go. But, O Davy! I wish to speak a few words to you first. I want to tell you what I heard dear father say to mother today." Minnie found it difficult to command her voice,— but she was determined to say what she had to say, though her brother looked a little impatient, as if afraid of a lecture. "Father said, 'I sometimes think I won't last long, Mary, and if I go, you'll have to give up the farm, as you'll have no son to help you.' "

"I hope that father is better than he thinks himself," said David, looking grave.

"I hope and trust that he is," faltered Minnie,

"but he has been so much pulled down by pain!"

"Yes, that makes him take care about this thing and that. I believe what ails him is more worry than anything else."

"And if a son could take off any of these cares, could prevent any of the worry, would it not be right—" began Minnie, but David impatiently cut her short. "Don't bother me about that,—I've made up my mind to go, and I'm going! Father hasn't thriven well as a farmer; I mean to thrive in some 'other line, and come back rich, and make you all comfortable and happy!"

There was a verse of Scripture in Minnie's mind, and she felt that she must repeat it, though it made her heart beat faster to do so, for she knew her brother's dislike of "religious talk." "Davy," she said very softly, " '*The blessing of the Lord, it maketh rich, and He addeth no sorrow with it.*' Can we look for that blessing if we turn away from our duty?"

"Minnie, it's a pity you're not a person; but I don't want sermons out of church!" cried David, half inclined to be angry, and yet aware in his con science that his sister was in the right. "Go and fetch me a bit of rope, will you,—and ask Jenny if the last shirt is ready. Come what may, nothing shall change me,—I'm off to London tomorrow!"

And so the lad set off on the following morning: and if a little sadness came over his heart as he received his mother's kiss and his father's blessing, and saw his sisters crying, it soon passed away. By the time that David had lost sight of the clump of elm-trees on the hill, and the church spire, which was a landmark for miles around, rising amongst them, and had crossed the little one-arch bridge which marked the boundary of the parish, his thoughts flowed as merrily and freely as the brook which sparkled below.

David found amusing companions in the train, whose talk beguiled the long journey to London. Great was his pleasure and excitement on arriving at the great bustling city, where everything was to him so new and so strange. David felt himself in a new world! He soon got into an omnibus and went off to the house of his uncle, the grocer, who had agreed to receive him, and put him into the way of earning an honest living.

The farmer's son did not much fancy the look of his new home, which was in rather a narrow, smoky street in the east end of London; he missed the clear air, the bright sunshine, the sweet scents to which he had been accustomed at Greenside. Nor was the 'lad much pleased with the manner and appearance of his uncle. Mr. White was a quiet, sober man of business, who went on year after year in the same routine of occupation, without himself requiring amusement or change, or ever thinking that others might require them.

His uncle, however, was kind to him; that is to say, he provided all that was needful for him, did not overwork his nephew, nor treat him with any harshness; but he naturally expected him to be punctual and steady, and do his allotted work.

David soon tired of this; he found that standing behind a counter, weighing out pounds of sugar and half pounds of tea, was no more exciting or amusing than threshing out corn in a barn. Besides this, David disliked the ways of his uncle's house; he could not bear the regular hours; he found the family prayer irksome, and he was angry at being warned against companions and amusements that were a great deal more to his taste.

"I can't stand this sort of thing!" said David to himself, after he had been but five days in London. Short as his visit had been, he had already managed to pick up acquaintance with three or four wild lads whom he fancied, as being "fellows up to a lark!" One of them put him in the way of getting another place, "Quite a different thing, a place where he wouldn't be hunted after by a prosing old Methodist uncle; where he would have the evenings and nights to spend as he pleased, and where he might be as jolly and free as ever he liked!"

David knew perfectly well that his parents would wish him to stay with his uncle White; that they would be uneasy if they knew him to be exposed to the numberless temptations of a great city, and seeking the society of such comrades as would only lead him into evil. Again, two paths lay before David Aspinall,—God's path of duty,—his own of self will. Again the lad turned *from* the right, in his careless pursuit after pleasure. He left his uncle, telling him that he thought he could "better himself" in another place; and that after giving it a trial, he was convinced that he never could settle down to the grocery business.

David soon found that he had indeed chosen a downward way; he would hardly have believed it possible, but a month before, that he could have made such quick progress in evil. The lad had always been careless and thoughtless as regarded religion, but he had not hitherto been *profane*, he had never uttered an oath in his life. He had behaved decently, both when at his father's home and when under the roof of his uncle. Now all restraint was removed, and David became like one of his God; less companions. He could laugh at what once would have made him blush. He never prayed, he never opened his Bible, he never entered the door of a church. He frequented the taverns, the theatres, and places of low amusement. Sunday excursions were his delight. His guilt was all the greater that he knew what was his duty. David did not care to write to his parents; he scarcely liked to remember them at all, for a pang of conscience would sometimes shoot through his soul, when the thought would come, "What would father say if he could see me now?" "Poor mother! if she knew what I am after, it would well-nigh break her heart!" David even hated the sight of letters from home, they always made him so dull; he often wished that his family did not know his address.

This career of folly and sin lasted almost to the end of that year, and then it was brought suddenly to a close. David and a party of his companions were returning from Greenwich one Sunday night, heated with drink, when they took to breaking windows, and insulting or knocking down peaceable citizens whom they met. Young Aspinall, indeed, took less part than the rest in the more serious mischief, but he was mixed up in the whole affair, and accordingly found himself, with the others, in the lock-up before morning.

It was a dreadful trial to the lad, who had by no means lost his sense of shame, to be brought to court on that Monday morning, and charged with breaking the law. Some delay occurred, due to the absence of an important witness, and David was remanded till the next day, so he had to spend another miserable night in the company of pick-pockets and drunkards.

But if he had been wretched on his first appearance before a magistrate, David was far more wretched on his second, for as the prisoner entered the crowded, sweltering court, and raised his eyes for a moment (for he had hitherto kept them bent on the floor), they fell on the form of his father leaning on his crutch, his honest face looking old and haggard, and with such an expression of grief and shame upon it that it cut David to the soul.

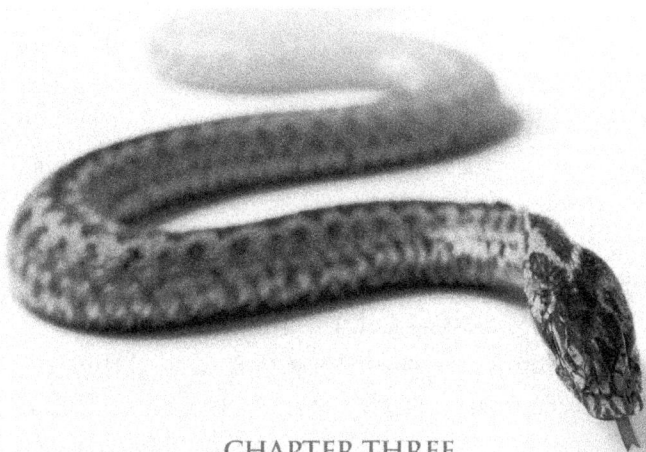

CHAPTER THREE

WANDERINGS—CONTINUED

JOHN ASPINALL had come up by the night train to London—a place which he had never visited before—on account of a telegram received from Mr. White on the preceding day at Greenside Farm. Never before had a telegram been seen, or scarcely heard of, in that quiet secluded spot, and its contents had filled the hitherto peaceful home with mourning and woe. Had the tidings been those of David's death, they would not have caused more anguish. His sisters cried bitterly, little Nelly the loudest of all, though she could not, of course, understand the cause of the trouble; she only knew that something dreadful had happened to Davy.

Jenny was indignant at the thought of her brother—her darling brother—being brought before a magistrate. "He is as innocent as a lamb, I'm certain that he is," she exclaimed through her sobs. "This is the doing of some wicked, cruel enemy, who wants to ruin our Davy. Are you not sure that he is innocent, Minnie?"

Poor Minnie could only hope so. Her love was as tender as Jenny's, but not so blind. She was too well aware that poor Davy had not made duty the rule of his conduct at home, and she knew that when a stone is set rolling down a steep hill, no one can tell where it will stop. The tone of the very few short notes which David had written home during the last six months had made his sister very uneasy; of late he had written none at all. Minnie was less surprised than distressed when the sad news came. She tried, though with a very sore heart, to cheer her mother, and speak hope to her father, but her great resource was pouring out her heart in prayer to God.

Mrs. Aspinall could not weep, and would not complain; but she trembled, and a feeling of faint sickness came over her frame. Her boy, her darling, her pride, he to whom she had once looked as her future comfort and the support of the family, was he to bring down the grey hairs of his parents with sorrow to the grave?"

"Wife," said the farmer abruptly, "I must be up to London; there's a train starts at ten tonight."

Mrs. Aspinall cast a sad look out at the chill wintry landscape, but she knew it would be vain to attempt to prevent her husband from taking the journey. She pulled out of her pocket a purse, for she usually had charge of the money of the family.

She emptied the purse on the table with her cold trembling fingers; there were a few small pieces of silver, and several of copper, but *not* one of gold.

The farmer looked at the meager store for a moment or two with a knitted brow, then muttered as if to himself, "Cobbs said last week how he'd be glad to buy Crummie;—I'll just step over and see if he's in the same mind."

"We'd spare anything for our boy," said Mary Aspinall. These were the first words which she had trusted herself to utter since the arrival of that dreadful telegram. So Crummie was sold, the favorite family cow that the farmer had reared from a calf; that had been the pride and pet of his children, and whose milk had been the chief means, as his wife often said, of bringing him through his long illness.

So with a full purse but a fuller heart the unhappy father started on his journey to London, on a dark, cold, drizzly night. He would not have ventured alone, for Mary yearned to go with him, except Mrs. Aspinall feared that all the spare cash would be needed for David, and she felt that it was necessary for Mary to take care of the girls and the farm.

After once catching a glimpse of his father in the courtroom, David could hardly give his mind to attend to what was passing around him. The voices sounded like a confused babble in his ears; he seemed conscious only of one thing, that he was a guilty wretch, deserving any amount of punishment that might be inflicted upon him. How had he repaid all the love that had been lavished on him since his birth; how had he fulfilled the fond hopes of which he had long been the object?

David Aspinall was convicted of a misdemeanor; the sentence was fine or imprisonment. John paid the fine at once; his son, who was well aware how scanty were the means of his parents, could not bear to think, though he could easily guess, how the money had been obtained. His uncle White, who was present, led the unhappy father, and even more unhappy son, out of the court, called a cab, and took them at once to his home. Not a word was uttered during the long rattling drive. The farmer sat opposite to David, leaning both hands on his crutch, with his head bowed down; a heavier weight than that of years was crushing the honest man to the dust!

Only then could David realize to some extent the misery described in the words of the Psalmist, the anguish of remorse without confession, remorse uncheered by the hope of God's forgiveness. The Lord's hand was heavy upon him; his moisture was indeed *changed into the drought of summer!*

David made a common mistake at this time of shame and anguish; he thought that *remorse* was *repentance*; he hated himself for his sin; but he had yet to learn that to *hate self* is not always to *give up self*, and that the heart may be wrung with misery, yet the stubborn will remain unbroken.

"You'll come back with me, lad? Your mother won't rest easy till she sees your face; and you're wanted more than ever at the farm." These were the first words which John Aspinall addressed on that day to his son, and they were uttered in a hoarse, husky voice.

"I'll never go back!" exclaimed David, with passionate excitement. "This will be known all over the village—I could not look anyone in the face! No, no; I'd sooner die than go back!"

"But what if it be your duty to go," said Mr. White, in a tone of grave reproof. "We must sometimes put our likes and dislikes out of the question, and try—to make up for the past."

"I'll go out to one of the colonies, and work my way in a place where I am not known," exclaimed David, who had hardly listened to his uncle, and who dared not look at his father.

Yet again the two ways, the right and the wrong, were before the young lad. Had his been true godly repentance, he would at any cost have tried to make the only amends that he could make to his family for all the grief that he had caused them. He would have sacrificed his self-will to what he knew to be the clear duty before him. He would have obeyed the wishes of his earthly father, and so have followed the guidance of his heavenly Father. But David was not prepared to do this. Once again, after all the bitter lessons of the past, he chose the way of his own inclination, and decided on working his way out to the African coast.

David did not even go back with his afflict-
ed father to spend Christmas at Greenside Farm;
he would not have done so even if he could have
afforded the expense of the journey; as it was, all his
wages had gone to selfish pleasures, and he had to
borrow from his uncle what was required for bare
necessaries to fit him out for the voyage.

Before a fortnight had passed, David was
tossing in the British Channel, encountering the
hardships of life at sea, and in vain straining his
eyes, as he passed the Dorsetshire coast, to catch a
glimpse of the distant church spire rising from the
clump of old elms.

The way of transgressors is hard. This is declared
in the Bible, and millions, by sad experience,
can testify to its truth. Everyone who habitually
chooses to follow his own will, disregarding duty
and conscience, will find in the end—if he find not
at once—that sorrow follows as the shadow of sin.
David was no longer a thoughtless, light-hearted
lad, he was a burdened sinner, ashamed to think of
his home, afraid to think of his God!

After a *miserable* voyage, which had seemed to
him as if it would never end, David arrived at the
Cape of Good Hope. He was almost penniless, and
did find it as easy as he had expected to obtain good
employment. He got a few odd jobs, but no per-
manent position. After a while he was tempted by
the offer of high wages, and also by the hope of adventure and sport, to go a considerable way inland,

to enter the service of Hans Kuhe, the Dutch Boer, whom I have already introduced to you.

The lad spent all that remained of his purse in making the long journey, and then found himself at Heinbok Kloof in the position almost of a prisoner, or rather of a slave, to the coarse-minded hard-hearted man whom he had chosen as master. David had no power to get away, for it was impossible for him, without money or oxen, to return to Cape Town through a dry barren tract, the haunt of wild beasts, and of tribes of nearly wild natives. Young Aspinall was chained to the service of one who so disliked England and the English that he gave the name of "Britain" to his most obstinate ox, for the express purpose of having something to thrash which bore that hated name.

Oh, how bitterly did David contrast the rude dwelling of Hans, seen under the glaring furnace of an African sun, to his own peaceful home in the valley; and the yellow thick-lipped Hottentots, who, whenever they could, left their work to be done by the English lad, to the dear ones whose faces and forms were so familiar to memory; his father, with his broad sun-burnt brow; his gentle mother, and his rosy-cheeked sisters. David even contrasted the lean long-legged oxen having sides scarred by the traces of the cruel rhinoceros hide whip, to the sleek cattle that grazed in English pastures, or stood, as he so often had seen them, in the pool enjoying the fresh cool waters in the stillness of a summer evening. Sorely did David repent that he had ever wandered from Greenside Farm.

Still, David's was not that repentance which leads the sinner to God, it was not laying down the burden of his sins and his sorrows at the feet of his Savior, and trusting to that Savior's mercy and merits for pardon and peace. It was not until that night on which this story opened, when David was returning from an expedition still further inland, undertaken by his master for purposes of barter with the natives, that the poor Wanderer had had a glimpse of the blessed truth that he might yet return to his heavenly Father, that his transgressions might be forgiven and all his sins blotted out.

Great as were his sufferings and dangers, that was a night of blessing to the penitent lad. It was then that he found his God and looked up to Him in faith, not as the stern Judge who would execute judgment upon a criminal, not as the awful King who would crush the rebel who had broken His laws, but as the compassionate Savior, deeply wronged, yet loving still, stretching forth those sacred hands once pierced for the sake of sinners, and calling to His wandering sheep, *"Turn ye, turn ye, why will ye die?"*

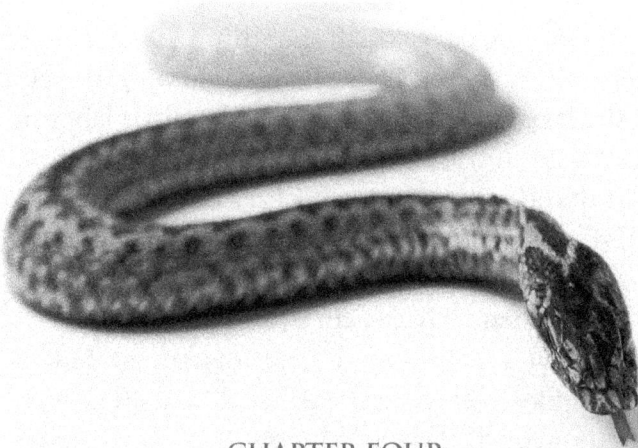

CHAPTER FOUR

FORSAKEN

"I acknowledged my sin unto Thee, and mine iniquity have I not hid. I said, I will confess my transgressions unto the Lord , and Thou forgivest the iniquity of my sin." —Psalm 32:5

"Up!—you *English* cur!" were the words, uttered in a harsh guttural tone of command, which awoke David from his short sweet dream, and roused him in a moment to a sense of the painful realities around him. "Up!—you *English* cur!" repeated the Boer, laying a stress on the word English so as to convey an insult in the sound. "Kick that fellow Pollux; these *Totties* (slang for the Hottentot people) are always eating or sleeping! We must yoke up the oxen and be off before the sun grows hot."

David sprang to his feet, but could hardly keep down an exclamation of pain as he did so, for so sharp was the pang which shot through his injured ankle. He, however, awoke Pollux, and with the help of the lazy Hottentot at once set about the labor of yoking the unwilling oxen. Hans, seated on the front part of the wagon, eating his breakfast meanwhile, and then smoking his pipe at ease, as he watched the efforts of his servants, which he tried to quicken now and then with an oath or a threat.

"How I hate and despise that man! how I should like to serve him out!" such had often been the thought of the English youth, and had sometimes been conveyed to its object in looks, if not in words; but on this morning there was something in the heart of David which softened the bitterness of his feelings even towards his tyrant.

The labor of yoking was rendered very severe by the pain which David suffered, and the sweat stood on his brow. He felt how impossible it would be for him to follow the wagon on foot, and when all was ready for a start, he limped up to his master,—

"Sir, you see how my ankle is swelled; I doubt whether I could walk a mile to save my life."

"Swelled,—I should think it was!" exclaimed the Boer; "why, you'll be no more use for the next month than a lame dog in hunting, or a lame ox in the yoke! What am I to make of you all that time, for you'll eat but you won't work?"

"I hope, sir, you'll let me sit on the wagon, you see that I cannot walk."

"Sit on my wagon, when those wretched beasts can hardly drag the load over the sand!" exclaimed the large heavy Boer, who had himself no intention of walking. "No, no, if you can't follow on foot, you may stay behind!" and the Dutchman put again into his mouth the pipe which he had taken out in order to speak, and pulled away in calm content, after uttering what was to his poor young servant almost like a sentence of death.

Commanding his voice and temper as well as he could, David made reply to his master, "You can hardly mean to leave me here, sir, in the midst of a desert, thirty miles from water, to perish by thirst, if not by wild beasts!"

"Pollux!—lash the oxen, and let us be off!" shouted the Boer.

"To leave me this way would be murder!" exclaimed David with indignation.

"You'll find your legs, I guarantee you, and follow the tracks of the wagon," observed Hans, as he resumed his pipe.

"At least—at least you will give me water—and a musket to defend myself from attacks of beasts, and to procure food—"

"Can't spare a musket—I only have three;—you may have that!" said the Boer, throwing down from the wagon a short spear of native make, on which he set little value, and which was likely to be of little use. "As for water," added the Boer, "I've just emptied the last drop from the cask."

So frightful was the fate to which the unfortunate youth was likely to meet, that limping painfully by the wagon, which was now in motion, he attemped by pleading to move the heart of his cruel master. David knew well that Hans had but to sacrifice a little of his property, to cast out of the wagon some of the heavy goods within, or go on foot himself, to enable him easily to give that help on which a life might depend. But Hans seemed as insensible to feelings either of honor or pity as the oxen which dragged him; and David, unable to keep up with the wagon, and in severe pain from the attempt to do so, was soon forced to fall behind.

He threw himself to the ground, and for some moments a feeling of sullen despair stole over the abandoned youth, as he listened to the creaking sound of the wheels, and the crack of the whip, and the shouting of Pollux growing fainter in the distance.

"My God—Oh, my God!" he murmured, "am I to perish here?"

David had never felt death so near, and he now tried to prepare his soul to look it calmly in the face. He might soon have to stand before his offended Maker—how should he appear? What plea could he offer for mercy? What hope had he that heaven would be his portion when he should lay down the weary burden of the flesh? David felt that his life was probably now to be counted by days, if not by hours; for on that most desolate route it was highly improbable that any human being would pass by to render aid. Time was precious indeed. Had David yet made his peace with God?

*A feeling of sullen despair stole over the abandoned youth,
as he listened to the creaking sound of the wheels.*

The first clear duty before the youth was to make humble confession of sin before God. As David lay on the sand, leaning his brow on his clasped hands, he reviewed in thought the events of his past life, trying his own conduct by the standard of God's commands. Had he loved the Lord his God with all his heart, his soul, and his strength? Nay, he had forgotten his Maker in the days of his youth—had broken His laws—had profaned His day—mocked at His people—slighted His word—even taken His name in vain! Had David done his duty towards his neighbor? Nay, he had treated with ingratitude and disobedience even the parents whom he loved; he had spoken many a word of anger; he had harbored thoughts of revenge; he had not indeed defrauded others of their due, for he had scorned dishonesty, but by his evil example he had encouraged others in sin. He had not kept his heart pure; he had not kept his lips clean; he had done what he ought not to have done, and left undone what he ought to have done, and from the depths of his soul the poor sinner confessed that there was no health in him.

The act of confession was in itself painful, and yet it brought a feeling of sweet relief. David had told God all—even as a child who has done wrong comes and confesses to a parent, feeling that any punishment is more tolerable than concealment would be. David had the blessed hope that his punishment, as regarded suffering for sin after death, had already been borne; that it had all been endured by the blessed Savior when He hung on the awful cross. "*There is no condemnation for them that are in Christ Jesus.*" Sin might indeed bring—had already brought—affliction in this present life. The psalmist was forgiven, yet tasted to the end of his days the bitter consequences of his sin; but very different is the correcting rod of a loving Father, who will make "*all things to work for good*" to His penitent child, from the crushing wrath of the Almighty descending upon a rebel who will not repent!

David's feelings at this time might be expressed in the following hymn which now recurred to his memory.

THE PENITENT'S HYMN

I dare not raise my guilty eye
The gaze of man to meet;
A helpless supplicant I lie,
Lord Jesus, at Thy feet!
Too justly scorned by all beside,
I to Thy mercy flee;
If Thou for "chief of sinners" died,
Is there no hope for me?

The weeping prodigal returned
His father's face to seek;
His supplication was not spurned,
Love still could welcome speak.
Like him, in grief and penitence,
Lord, to Thy cross I flee;
O Father, wilt Thou spurn me thence?
Is there no hope for me?

The dying thief in torments hung,
While sinners scoffed around;—
With fainting strength, and faltering tongue
He mercy sought and found!
There flowed before his eyeballs dim
The blood that set him free:
If Jesus heard and pitied him,
Is there no hope for me?

Yes, there is hope; while He, once crowned
With thorns, still reigns in heaven,
Rejoices o'er His lost one found,
His Wanderers forgiven;
To those who loathe and leave their sin
He offers mercy free;
I feel another life begin,—
There yet is hope for me!

After pouring out his heart in confession and prayer, David felt more calm, more resigned. He now raised himself a little and looked around. The prospect was indeed most desolate and dreary; and very painful was the reflected heat of the sun from the barren sands. There was scarcely a breath of air stirring, and what breeze came seemed to have passed through a furnace. David's mouth was parched and dry from thirst. He could see some wild creatures, probably zebras, galloping in the distance, but there was not the slightest chance of his being able to reach them; even had he possessed a musket, they would have been beyond its range. The only other object that in the least varied from the dreary sameness, was a patch of what seemed to be scarcely worthy of the name of vegetation, a few hundred yards to the left of the youth, and almost hidden from view by a little rise.

This patch looked so parched up and dry, that under other circumstances David would not have cared to go near enough to see what plants had found root in such a desolate place. Now, however, the shelter of even the smallest bush was not to be despised, and David, using the spear as a staff, slowly made his way over the rising ground towards the low clump. He was rewarded for the effort by a joyful surprise. With a delight which only those who have suffered from severe thirst can understand, David beheld a watermelon, large and juicy, lying on the ground—that plant which grows in African wastes, as if expressly designed by a gracious Providence to supply the want of water in a dry and parched land.

David seized the fruit with feverish haste, cut it open with a large clasp-knife which he carried about him, and partook with keen enjoyment its melting contents, which are said to relieve thirst even better than water. Nor was this all,—David had not been for months in the Damara land without learning the value of what, to a stranger's eye, might have looked like nothing but a few bare twigs. There was a treasure lying below, and David soon dug up with his spear a large juicy root wholesome and most refreshing, which is often eaten by the natives. These plants, growing in the wilderness, not only supplied the poor Wanderer's present need, but spoke a lesson of hope to his heart, like that which a little moss once taught the traveller Bruce. Here they grew in the lonely waste, living proofs of the care of an Almighty God, that unseen supplied their roots with nourishment, and made them live and spread where scarcely a blade of grass would otherwise grow.

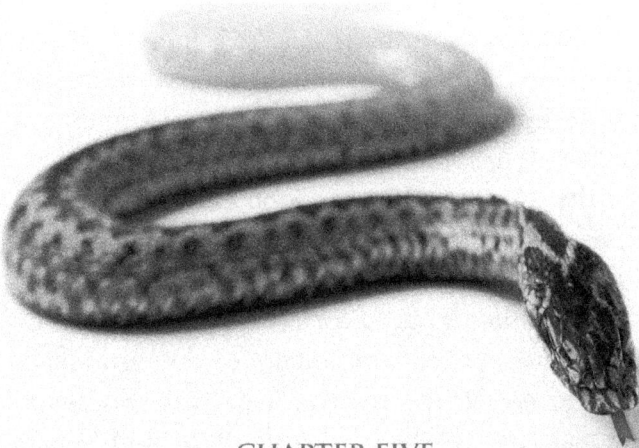

CHAPTER FIVE

NOT FORSAKEN

"For this shall every one that is godly pray unto Thee in a time when Thou mayest be found: surely in the floods of great waters they shall not come nigh unto him."—Psalm 32:6

DAVID was still thankfully partaking of the root called Markrohae, when his attention was arrested by the appearance, on the sandy horizon, of a four footed creature approaching towards him at full speed. He soon distinguished that it was a Springbok, a kind of antelope of the desert, moving rapidly forward in bounds such as perhaps no other four-footed animal can make. It was coming straight in his direction, and David crouched down low, grasping his spear, and hiding himself as well as he could behind the scraggy bushes. He was surprised to see a solitary individual of a species that generally travels in herds, and still more so that a creature so timid and shy should not have perceived him, so imperfectly concealed as he was, and have startled off in some other direction.

The cause for this was soon evident, as David perceived that three wild dogs were in hot pursuit of the Springbok, which they had probably singled out from a herd. The chase must have been a long and severe one, for the antelope was now slackening its speed, and the terrified creature was too much alarmed by the close pursuit behind to take notice of danger in front. Before it could reach the bushes the foremost dog had pulled it down by the neck, and in seconds the other two were on their now lifeless prey.

Now was the moment for David! With steady aim he sent his light spear whirling through the air and right amongst the ravenous wolf-like creatures that had just run down their quarry. It grazed the shoulder of one of the wild dogs, which yelped a cry of pain. David sprang to his feet, threw up his arms, and shouted!

Whether it was his sudden appearance, or the sound of a human voice, which is said to have a strange power over the beasts of which man was made the lord, is not needful to ponder. The savage creatures did not await the approach of the unarmed youth, but a second shout sent them galloping off with such speed as their already half exhausted strength would allow, flying from the face of man, and leaving their prey behind.

The chase must have been a long and severe one for the antelope was now slackening its speed.

"This is indeed wonderful!" murmured David, as he painfully limped over to the spot where the dead antelope lay. "God has made the very beasts of prey provide me food in the desert! *Thou preparest a table before me.* That is from the twenty-third Psalm. I can no longer say that it is not a Psalm for *me. Yea, though I walk through the valley of the shadow of death, I will fear no evil, for Thou art with me.* I will no longer think myself alone. Even after all my guilty wanderings, God has not forsaken me. I will trust Him in life and in death, *for His mercy endureth forever.*"

Using the spear again as his staff, David, with considerable difficulty, dragged the body of the dead Springbok to the small thicket where he had just been resting before the commotion. He had learned from the Bushmen their way of procuring fire without match, flint, or steel, and now his knowledge served him well. He first gathered together some leaves, which the fierce sun had made almost as dry as tinder; next he cut two sticks with his knife, making a small notch in the first, and sharpening the point of the second; he then put this point into the notch, and twirled the second stick round between the palms of his hands so rapidly, as to produce sufficient heat to set fire to the little dry heap. He threw on this some withered twigs, and soon a thin cloud of blue smoke curled up in the clear desert air.

David's cooking a portion of his antelope was very rough going, but he sat down to his hastily prepared meal with a very thankful heart. He had always been accustomed at Greenside Farm to hear his father "*say grace*" before dinner, but since leaving England, David had never himself thought of giving thanks for his food, until he partook of this meal which God had providentially spread before him in the desert. It was no longer a mere heartless form with which David uttered the words, "For these, and *all* His mercies, the Lord's name be praised!"

David was not only refreshed and strengthened by the food, but he was cheered by the thought that for one night at least he might be able to keep off attacks from wild beasts by lighting a fire. His supply of fuel was indeed very scanty, but then he would use it sparingly. He had not enough wood for the next day, but why be anxious for tomorrow? God had amply supplied the needs of today, He would not desert him then. David found occupation in gathering together materials for his evening fire, and then made up for his short broken rest by taking a refreshing afternoon sleep.

When the youth awoke he again partook of some food, and relieved his thirst by finishing what he had left of the melon from the morning. Then, reclining on the sand by the heap of dried sticks and leaves which he would light after sunset, David gave himself up to holy thoughts, repeating to himself the thirty-second Psalm, and dwelling upon its meaning verse by verse.

"*For this shall every one that is godly pray unto Thee.*" David paused that he might try better to understand this passage of Scripture.

"As this Psalm tells of mercy to him *whose transgression is forgiven, whose sin is covered*, I should have thought that the word would rather have been, 'For this shall every one that is *ungodly* pray unto Thee.' It is only they who want the mercy. But who are the godly, who are the *righteous* mentioned so often in the Bible? Do we not read in another part, '*There is none that doeth good, no, not one?*' Did not our Savior Himself say, '*There is none good but one, that is God?*' What is meant, then, by godly, and why should the godly pray *because* God has mercy on sinners?"

This was a difficult question, and David could not for a long time think of a satisfactory reply. Would not the Apostle Peter be counted "godly?" and yet Peter three times denied his Lord. Surely Paul was "righteous," yet he had been a persecutor of the early church and a blasphemer. At length the truth seemed to dawn upon David as the words recurred to his mind, "*In the Lord have I righteousness and strength.*" Surely the "godly" in the sixth verse of the Psalm must be the very same as the "blessed one" mentioned in the first, "*whose transgression is forgiven, whose sin is covered,*" who is counted righteous before God; because, through faith, he is made a partaker of the spotless righteousness of Christ. It is to such that it is said in the Psalm, "*The Lord imputeth not iniquity*". Yes, the "godly" is not, cannot be the man who has committed no sin, for in that case there would be none godly upon earth; but rather he that loveth much, because he hath been much forgiven!

"Now I remember," thought David, "the large picture of the Deluge, which used to hang between the two lattice windows in my dear old room at Greenside, and what my mother said to us about it on one wintry Sunday, when we were almost blocked up by snow." David sighed heavily as he recalled the bright blaze of the wood-fire, rendered so welcome by the sharp keen air, and how those lattice windows had been all feathery with frost, and the trees without silvered with frozen dew. To the poor Wanderer, half burnt up by African heat, ice and snow and sharp crisp air seemed the greatest of luxuries.

David went on with his train of thought in reference to the picture of the Deluge. "My dear mother pointed out to us the Ark floating on the surface of the waters, while the rain poured in torrents from the sky, and poor wretches were drowning even on the tops of the highest hills. "Mind you, my children," she said, "the family of Noah were safe, *not* because they were good swimmers or good sailors, but *just* because they had faith and obedience to make them go into the Ark. *That* was the place of safety which God had provided, and *no other* was safe. And so Christ is our Ark and our

Refuge now. If we are in Him we are safe; even at the last awful day the great waters of destruction shall not come nigh us!"

And what is it to be *in Christ*? Is it not to come to Him as a poor, helpless, perishing sinner, whose only hope is in His mercy? Has He not said of such, *He that cometh unto me I will in nowise cast out*?

Reader, I ask you not whether you have ever been a wanderer like David, or whether you have led what men may call a blameless life. I ask, have you ever come to Christ; have you given your heart to Him? If so, He is willing, ready to clothe you with His own righteousness, to give you His Spirit to make you holy, and render you, by that Spirit's power, one of the "godly" that pray unto Him!

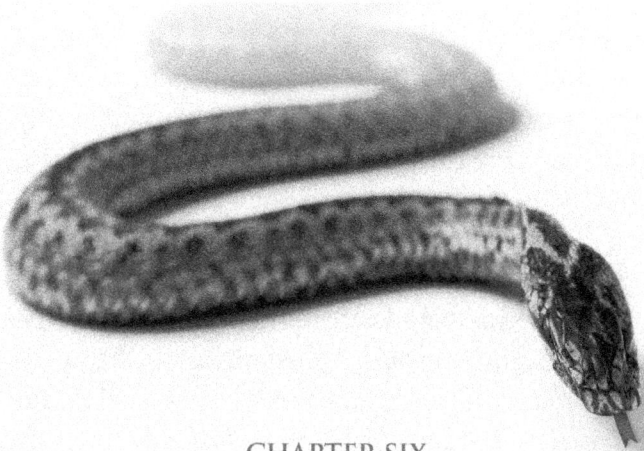

CHAPTER SIX

PERIL AT HAND

"Thou art my hiding-place; Thou shalt preserve me from trouble; Thou shalt compass me about with songs of deliverance." —Psalm 32:7

THE glowing red sun went down, just as David, after much difficulty, had succeeded in kindling his small dry heap of firewood. There was little or no twilight; in a short time all was dark (for the moon had not yet risen), except when the English youth, on his lonely watch, carefully placed one crackling branch after another upon his little fire.

"I must not go to sleep," thought David, "or my fire will go out, especially as I dare not waste my precious fuel to make it large enough to last without constant care. The desert seems to me to be more than usually still: even the jackals are silent, and I cannot hear the hyena's horrible laugh!" David put his ear close to the ground to listen, and then,—even on that sultry night and close to a fire,—there came over him a feeling like a chill, and he hastily threw on more fuel, and made the flames leap high, while he looked anxiously in one particular direction, and then bent down again and listened.

"Yes, I could not mistake that sound, though uttered, perhaps, miles from hence! That was the roar of the lion himself! I must not allow the fire to die down, for that is my only protection now, except the mercy—the watchful care of my God!"

It was no small comfort to David to feel the night-breeze blowing from the direction in which he had heard the roar,—for as he was downwind of the lion, the terrible king of the desert was not so likely to scent either him or the remains of the Springbok which he was heating at the fire. Still it was an awful position for him; alone in the waste, with the knowledge that a fierce wild beast was roaming abroad, and that there was not so much as the barrier of a wall or a hedge between it and him! It was somewhat natural that David, in this strange peril, should recall to mind a verse from Peter's epistle—"*Be sober, be vigilant; be cause your adversary, the Devil, as a roaring lion, walketh about, seeking whom he may devour.*"

"How much more carefully, how much more anxiously I guard against the lion which can only destroy my body, than I did against him who so nearly destroyed my soul!" thought David. "Here am I now, giving up sleep, treasuring every dry stick as if it were worth its weight in gold, stirring my fire to a blaze, listening, watching, waiting, ready to jump up at any moment with my spear in my hand! How was it with me in my careless days of sin? Why, I have profanely laughed at the notion of danger; I have been angry at warnings, however wisely given; I have scarcely believed that there was a Devil at all, and I have actually jested with the soul-destroyer's name on my lips! I was no more afraid of the Lion that goes about seeking to devour, than this *dead* Springbok is of the fierce wild beast that may swallow it up in a moment. And why was I so easy and careless? It was because *I was dead in sin*; my conscience was dead! Thank God, the God of mercy, that I did not then perish for ever,—called to the bar of judgment unrepenting, and therefore unforgiven!"

For hours the Wanderer sat feeding his fire, while the full moonlight fell around him, and thousands of twinkling stars glimmered in the deep blue sky above. The fire, kept up to scare away lions and other beasts of prey, was like the grace of God in the heart, which every Christian must carefully tend by watchfulness and prayer. Oh! dear reader, when we find our hearts growing cold towards God; when our light does *not* shine before men; when we become sleepy and careless in religion, let us tremble and rouse ourselves to greater vigilance. *For our enemy is not asleep*; temptation and danger are near; far greater peril than any that can threaten the body alone!

Sometimes David fancied that he saw dim forms, like shadows, moving in the distance; and once again, but still afar off, he heard the sound of the deep low roar which strikes such terror to the heart. He tried to keep his soul calm and composed, trusting in God;—to realize the precious assurance contained in the words of the Savior: *Are not jive sparrows sold for two farthings, and not one of them is forgotten before God? But even the very hairs of your head are all numbered. Fear not, therefore; ye are of more value than many sparrows.* Who should be so fearless as the Christian who rests under the shadow of the Almighty's wings? Of what need he be afraid to whom death itself, whenever or howsoever it come, is but a messenger of love to hear him to the presence of a Father!

Though David found comfort in such thoughts, he was thankful when the long, long night was gone away; though, oh, how slowly! At length a glow appeared in the eastern sky, the morning broke at last, and there was the Wanderer, alive and unharmed.

How much during the night had David thought of his home and every individual in it; memory calling up each dear familiar face, till he could almost fancy himself again seated with his family round the cheerful table, with little Nelly on his knee. And how fondly he had prayed for everyone at Greenside:—his good father, his tender mother, the sisters who had been his playmates and friends! What earnest resolutions David had made, that if God should please to spare his life, and let him return to England, he would be the comfort and help of his parents, a true brother and guardian to the girls. How cheerfully would he labor, not for a cruel master, but for a loving father; not as a bondsman, but as a son! And even in such a spirit would he try to work for his God. His service should not be that of slavish fear, but of grateful adoring love! He would think no duty too hard, no duty too painful, if called to do it for the sake of his merciful Savior!

It was now broad daylight, the sun had risen, and David beheld with surprise the change in the scene before him. Not half a mile distant appeared at large and beautiful lake, reflecting like a polished mirror the glittering sunshine! Here and there a soft isle appeared to dot the blue expanse of the waters. The scene was lovely, and all the more so as contrasted with the barren wildness of that upon which the sun had set on the preceding evening. David gazed with admiration indeed, but not with a pleasure. He knew that he looked upon a mirage, that all was as false as it was fair; that with that shining lake before him he might yet perish with thirst! Wide as the waters appeared, the Wanderer knew that there was not a drop of real moisture with which he could cool his burning lips, and he would have thankfully exchanged all the goodly show for a single cup of cold water!

"Ah!" said David to himself, with a sigh, "had I but reached this spot at night, and so not have known but too well the nature of the country around, with what eager hope and delight the sight of that lake would have filled me! How, at the cost of any pain, I would have rushed towards it, from the longing to plunge myself into its cool refreshing waters! In the days of my ignorance it was thus that I looked upon sinful pleasure; *it was a mirage* to my soul; I must and would reach it, and no one should keep me back! I had what I resolved to obtain, and what did I find? not cooling waters, but barren sand! Oh! how much of sorrow was needed to teach me the lesson that the soul's thirst for happiness cannot be quenched by the world's mirage! It can only be satisfied by the love of Him who said, *He that believeth on Me shall never thirst.*

David had imagined that with the night his greatest danger from wild beasts would pass away, that whatever his sufferings might be from its heat, at least some degree of safety would come from the sun. But when, after watching the mirage for some time, he chanced to turn his eyes in a different direction, he started in sudden alarm! What is that coming towards him?—a single creature, and a large one; it is neither giraffe nor zebra! David, alone and unprotected, felt his heart throb fast at the suspicion which flashed across his mind as to the nature of the creature that came on so rapidly over the sand! It was not long that he could cling to a doubt, it was a large lion that was galloping towards him, and it saw him; for straight as an arrow it came in the Wanderer's direction!

David kept his eyes fixed on the lion; and the glaring eyes of the lion were fixed upon him.

The wild beast slackened its pace as it drew nearer; the bounding gallop was changed to a crouching walk; David would willingly at that moment have given his left hand to have had a double-barrelled gun in his right. For well he knew that his small spear would be of little use in a struggle with an enemy so powerful as the desert king. He would not attempt to fling the weapon, it would only serve to irritate, not to inflict a mortal wound.

It was a fearful thing to stand watching the gradual approach of the lion, and yet David was calmer and more resolute than under circumstances far less trying to flesh and blood. Even at that awful time there was a sense of the presence of God, which strengthened his soul to meet danger, and, if needs be, death itself as a man and a Christian should meet them!

David kept his eyes fixed on the lion; and the glaring eyes of the lion were fixed upon him. The youth had often heard tales amongst Hottentots of adventures with wild beasts in which the power of the human eye had been mentioned, and when it had been said that even the lion fears to attack a man who looks him full in the face. David had not put much faith in such stories, but had often said that he believed the best use of the eye in such cases was to direct a heavy bullet aright. But the young Englishman had now no other resource, and he dared scarcely so much as let an eyelid quiver, as he surveyed the lion with so fixed a stare that a dimness seemed to come over his sight from the intensity of his gaze. As if half spellbound, more and more slowly advanced the lion, crouching cat-like on the sand, lashing his tawny tail, and uttering continuously,—a low fierce growl!

Five, ten minutes thus passed—every minute seemed an hour: suspense became almost intolerable; but the end appeared now to be at hand. The lion was not many yards from the English youth, and suddenly, with an angry shake of his mane, drew himself together in the act to spring! At this instant a sharp report rang through the air, then another, and another,—and almost before the dizzied brain of David could realize the fact that rescuers must be near, the lion, with a last wild roar of agony and rage, rolled over on the sand, and lay quivering in death but a few paces from the feet of its intended victim.

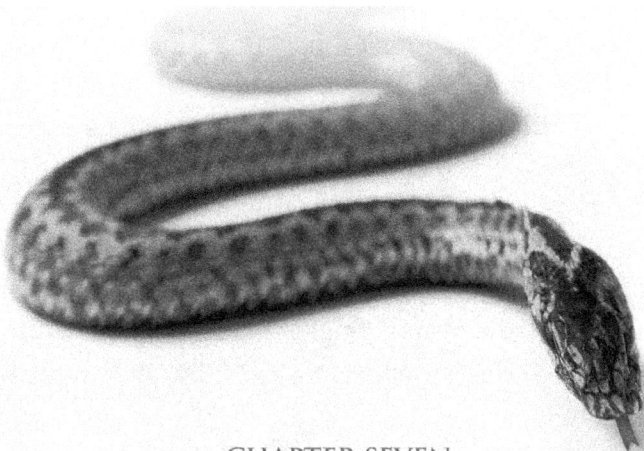

CHAPTER SEVEN

RESOLUTIONS

"I will instruct the: and teach thee in the way which thou shalt go: I will guide thee with mine eye." —Psalm 32:8

"A RIGHT good shot, and a splendid prize!" exclaimed a loud cheerful voice in English, as, musket in hand, a young mounted hunter galloped up to the spot, followed by another, a few years older than himself, whose face, bearded and bronzed, was unmistakably English.

"You've had a narrow escape!" cried the second rider to David, who still stood as if rooted to the ground.

"A merciful deliverance!" gasped the youth.

"Aye, a merciful deliverance indeed!" repeated the first rider, whose name was Carlton. "We had to make a circuit to get a fair broadside shot, and feared, every moment, that the beast would spring on you before we got near enough to take a sure aim. I had to fire at last at so long a range, that I scarcely expected the bullet would strike. What a splendid creature this lion is, Manners! Of all our hunting spoils, this is the noblest by far!" And dismounting, the young Englishman surveyed with admiration the immense carcass of the once formidable lion.

"You are a lad of mettle!" observed Manners to David; "you stood your ground like a hero!"

"I could neither fight nor make flight," answered David simply, "or I'd have been glad enough to do either."

"How came you,—and without a gun,—to be here all alone in such a wild place as this?" asked Carlton with some curiosity and interest.

"I served Hans Kuhe, the Boer, the track of whose waggon you may see yonder. I fell lame; he would not let me ride, and I could not walk,— and so he left me behind."

"The brute!" exclaimed the young hunter.

"Notwithstanding your lameness, you seem to have had some luck in hunting," observed Manners, glancing at what remained of the Springbok.

"I could not follow the game,—the game was sent to me," answered David, his heart glowing with gratitude as he spoke; "wild dogs pulled it down near to this spot, and with my spear I was able to frighten them away, and take what God had provided. It was He, too, who brought you here, gentlemen—you to Whom I owe my life, for which I thank you from the depths of my soul!"

"We were but just in time," observed Manners.

Carlton had already begun a rough measurement of the lion, which was one of the largest size,— and he conversed eagerly as he went on with his occupation.

"This king of beasts—he deserves the name—has led us a good chase this morning over his desert domain. He was prowling last night round the spot where we had camped, and made our oxen half mad with terror; but I suppose he thought discretion the better part of valor, for he did not venture on an attack, and made off before we could get a fair shot. We mounted, and have been following on his trail ever since there was light enough to see it; but I doubt whether we should ever have come up with our game, had you not headed him, and kept him at bay. You are certainly the hero of this lion adventure, and deserve the tail as a trophy."

"You will, of course, join our party," said Mr. Manners kindly to David; "our wagons will be up in an hour or so, for we intend to camp tonight at Quagga Fountain."

"And Manner will play surgeon to your injury," said Carlton gaily; "he is doctor-in-chief to our party, and can set a bone or "cut off a leg in a twinkling!"

David joyfully accepted the offers of his fellow countrymen. The sound of his native tongue, in its purity, was as music to his ears, and the frank, cordial kindness which he met with was all the more delightful especially in contrast to the harsh conduct he had received at the hands of the Boer. How marvelously had the Wanderer been watched over and cared for;—to the hungry, food had been sent; to the friendless, friends; and to the helpless, great deliverance! It sweetened every blessing to David, to regard it as coming directly from God. Thankfulness is the parent of cheerfulness. We may safely affirm, that he who has a heart to praise will never lack something to praise for.

The hunters now proposed galloping back to their wagons, and sending some of the "Totties" to help to skin the lion.

"And probably feast on the carcass," laughed Carlton. "So that they can have plenty of flesh, these fellows are not particular as to what it comes from."

"Shall I take you up behind me on my horse?" said Manners to David.

David declined the kindly offer, the state of his ankle being such as would have rendered the ride extremely painful; besides, he was unwilling to cause inconvenience to one of his preservers. He would rather remain where he was, he said, and watch by the dead lion until the wagons came up.

"I'll just load my gun and leave it with you,

then," said Manners; "you might have other unpleasant visitors while left alone here."

"And we'll not forget to send you, by the Totties, something to help your breakfast," added Carlton; "you have plenty to eat, as I see, but the liquor must not be wanting."

In few but fervent words David again thanked his new friends, who did not care to wait to be thanked. Off they rode, blithe and merry, joyful at having slain their lion, and still more delighted at having been the means of saving a gallant lad from a terrible fate.

Once more was David left to himself, and solitude was not unwelcome, for with it he could more freely pour out his heart's deep thanksgiving to God. He could also more quietly form resolutions for the future. He would now plead for the fulfillment of that gracious promise contained in his mother's favorite Psalm, "*I will instruct thee and teach thee in the way which thou shalt go.*" David resolved that from that day forth he would never take any important step in life without praying for heavenly guidance; nor would he—God's Spirit helping his resolve—ever suffer his own wayward will to draw him from the straight path.

"What is meant by *I will guide thee with mine eye?*" David reflected on the expression. It is always well to ponder over such passages until their full meaning becomes clear to our minds.

"I remember," thought young Aspinall, "that when Minnie and I were children together, mother gave an account of our behavior during his absence to father, who had been on business away from home three days. 'I've had a little trouble with Davy,' she said (I daresay that it was *not a little*), 'for he does not always mind what is said to him; but as for my little Minnie, a *look* is enough for her. Minnie was so obedient to her mother that she could be guided by *the eye*. That must be the meaning of those words in the Psalm, and what a beautiful meaning it is! I have been through life like a willful, disobedient child, and God has had to draw me back to Himself by means that were rough and painful. I have had shame and less, pain and danger, and all these trials were needed, not one could have been spared me. It would not have been thus with me if I had obeyed from the first the voice of conscience within. Yes, *Conscience* applying Scripture must be the *directing look* of the Lord; and the man who follows it fully and faithfully, 'he it is whom God *guides by His eye.*"

The greatest earthly desire David now had was to return to his home and fulfill those wishes of his parents, which had now become his own. Even the recollection of the painful passage in his life in London which had once made him so shrink from going back to Greenside was now insufficient to damp that desire. The thought of treading again the well-known fields, and hearing the dear familiar voices,—climbing the orchard—trees in autumn, and tossing down sweet apples to Eliza, whose good humored face would look almost as round and rosy as they,—or sitting by the fire, on winter evenings, telling tales of African life,—how delightful would this be! Then the walk with his father and mother along the green lanes to the church on the hill, with Jenny close at his side; or listening to the soft music of Minnie's voice teaching Nelly the evening hymn—all was like a dream of happiness to the poor Wanderer in Africa, too bright to be ever realized!

But how could David get back to England? Doubtless the generous hunters who had already shown so much kindness would take him in safety to some part of the colony where he would at least be in no danger of starvation, or of perishing by attacks of beasts, or Bushmen. But David felt that he had no right to expect anything more from them. The injury to his ankle was so severe that he feared it would be long indeed before he could have a chance of working his way home; and though, at the Cape, he might earn something by the labor of his hands, he knew from experience that such a long space of time must elapse before he could save up enough to pay for a passage to England, that he could barely contemplate it. In the meantime what might not happen! David was in a feverish state from heat, thirst, and the pain in his ankle. It is likely, too, that the adventure with the lion had, for the time, shaken his nerves; indeed, to face such a fearful creature alone, and for so long a time, was enough to try the firmest;—all these causes together produced a depressing effect upon his spirits. A horrible fear came over him that he should never see his father again, never be able to ask his forgiveness, that he should arrive in England just too late, and find the farm in the hands of strangers, his family gone, nothing of theirs left but a new tombstone in the churchyard!

David groaned aloud as his feverish fancy presented all this to his mind with the vividness of reality. Oh, that he had wings to fly home! How could he endure to wait for months, perhaps for years, before he could embark for Old England! Could it be wrong to wish, to pray for money, when money could take him to his home? David did pray, and very earnestly, that the way might be opened before him, and that his father might be spared to rejoice in his prodigal's return.

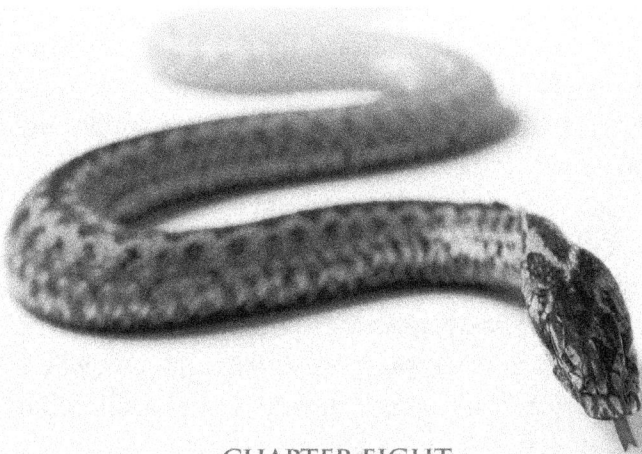

CHAPTER EIGHT

GUIDANCE

"I will guide thee by mine eye."—Psalm 32:8

THE movements of the two wagons belonging to the English hunters, though certainly quicker than those of the Boer, who had lost so many of his span, (about 14 oxen) were tedious to the impatient David. He did not, however, have to remain suffering from thirst until they came up, for a party of Hottentots, sent by the hunters, who were themselves engaged in shooting, came up to carry off the skin and claws of the lion, and Manners had not forgotten to forward by them water, and other things needful to him.

David, though to a certain degree refreshed; longed for the shelter of the wagon to shield him from the blazing sun. He was not exactly in the track along which the wagons would pass; having left it, as the reader is aware, for the little low clump of bushes. David, to whom the sight and scent of the Hottentots engaged in their task were anything but agreeable, took the musket and spear to support his painful steps, and made his way back to the road, if a road it could be called, where he saw on the sand the broad marks of the wheels of Hans' wagon, and the hoof-prints of his weary oxen. The youth was now not many yards from the spot where he had pleaded, though in vain, to be taken up on that wagon,—perhaps some fifty paces farther on the road than where he had stood at that time. Emotions of fiery indignation rose in the Wanderer's breast, when he thought of the cruel wrong that had been done him, and how nearly the conduct of his heartless master had given him over as a prey to the lion.

David was turning over these reflections in his mind, when his eye chanced to fall on an object lying not far from his feet, on the track of the Boer's wagon. He knew in an instant what it was, and, hastening to the spot, as fast as pain would let him, he raised from the sand a large leather purse, heavy with gold, that gold which Hans Kuhe prized more than anything else upon earth, except, perhaps, his brandy-flask and his pipe.

A crowd of conflicting feelings pressed upon the mind of David as he grasped the heavy purse, dropped on the road by the man who had almost been his murderer. The very first thought which arose was, "This is sent in answer to prayer; this money will take me home!" Then there followed a strange conflict within, a kind of dialogue which David held with his own soul; or rather, there was the Tempter of man speaking on the one hand, and Conscience answering on the other. If the reader knows nothing of such an inward struggle, it is to be feared that it is because Conscience is silent, not because sin is dead.

TEMPTER.—Why should you doubt for a moment whether it is lawful for you to take this money which Providence has placed in your very path?

CONSCIENCE.—It is written, "*Thou shalt not covet*;"—"*Thou shalt not steal.*"

TEMPTER.—The hateful Boer owes you wages; it is lawful to take your own.

CONSCIENCE.—He owes you but *one* piece of gold, which alone can be rightfully yours; that purse, by its weight, contains at least forty.

TEMPTER.—But think of the good you might do; with that money. In the hands of the Boer it will be spent on drunken revels, or still worse. With you it will make your parents happy; it will take you back to the home which it was sin in you ever to leave.

CONSCIENCE.—How that money will be spent by another is not the point to decide. It is not the Boer's conduct, but your own, that *you* must answer for before God. "*Ill-gotten wealth brings no blessing, but a curse.*" "*Let none do evil, that good may come.*"

TEMPTER.—But think on your cruel wrongs. Remember the insulting words,—nay, even the blows which you have had to endure. Think on the barbarity of him who could leave a faithful follower to die a lingering death, and that, too, from a hurt received in his service. If you cannot keep the purse for yourself, throw it away; let it be found by someone else who will use the money without a scruple. Take out the one piece, which is your own, and then scatter the gold to the right and the left. You may scorn to keep another man's money, but you may enjoy the 'sweetness of revenge.' Your tyrant will have to bear a heavy loss, and it is to be hoped that he will look upon it as a just punishment for his conduct to you.

CONSCIENCE.—It is written, "*Do good to them that hate you; pray for them that despitefully use you and persecute you.*" It is written, "*If ye do not forgive, neither will your Father which is in; Heaven forgive your trespasses.*" There is a safe and simple rule which every servant of Christ is to follow, "*Be not overcome of evil, but overcome evil with good.*"

Conscience had won the victory, and David enjoyed the blessed experience of what it is for God's child to be guided by His eye.

The youth resolved to restore the purse, at the first opportunity, to its rightful owner; but human nature is weak, and he knew that if such opportunity were long delayed, the temptation which he had just conquered might come back again irresistible force. Reason told him that it would be better to put it out of his power to take from that store of gold in case his need should be very dire or a great length of time should elapse before he should meet Hans Kuhe again. The Beer was, as David believed, more than a day's march before him, and his road would turn off at Quagga Fountain in quite a different direction from that which the English party were likely to take. The gentlemen would know better than David could how to send money across a wild country; the lad therefore made up his mind to place the purse in their hands, after taking from it the small amount of wages actually due to himself.

Before the hunters came riding up towards him a little in advance of their wagons, David had decided on the right course to be pursued. As soon as they had dismounted and had come up to place where he was awaiting their arrival, young Aspinall gave the purse into the hands of Manners, and told him that he had picked it up on the road, but that he knew it belonged to Hans Kuhe, a Dutch Boer, who lived at Heinbok Kloof, and that he hoped the gentlemen would kindly take charge of it, and have it restored to its owner.

"How came you to identify a common-looking purse so readily?" inquired Mr. Carlton.

"I have seen it dozens of times in the hands of its owner; I know well that tobacco-stain left by his fingers."

"He is some friend of yours then, I suppose?"

"Hardly to be called so," answered David with a smile; "only yesterday he was my master."

"Your master!" exclaimed Carlton; "what—the fellow who left you to die in the desert!"

Carlton whistled, and turned on his heel. Manners smiled, placed the heavy purse in one of his pockets, and told David that he would take care not only that it should reach its owner, but that the Boer should be informed who had been its finder.

"And now, my boy," said the Englishman, "let me play the surgeon, and look at your ankle."

Very skillfully and very kindly did Manners, like the good Samaritan, bind up the hurt of the young traveler whom he had met by the way, Carlton looking on with interest as he did so. The three then mounted the wagon, whose canopy, lined with many a trophy of the chase, offered a refreshing shelter from the blazing heat of noon. Manners made David rest on his own bed in the wagon, where the lad enjoyed a long deep sleep, from which he awoke quite free from fever, and much more disposed to look upon everything in a cheerful light.

It was very pleasant indeed to David, who had been treated as a dog by Hans Kuhe, to find himself not only in the society of countrymen and gentlemen, but to be aware that they were both very favorably disposed towards him, and that they admired his courage and honesty. It was not merely the hope that Manners and Carlton might in some way help his return to England that made this knowledge so delightful to David; he had a heart that warmed to kindness, especially in a foreign land, and after having experienced so much of the reverse, the youth was naturally desirous to keep the good opinion of the hunters, and was anxious not to say or do anything which might lower him in their eyes.

As the three sat in the wagon together, the gentlemen asked David a few questions as to his parentage and birthplace, and seemed pleased when they heard that he was the son of an English farmer.

"One might have guessed that you harken from the race of our bold countrymen," observed Carlton, "when you would face a lion for half an hour without blinking!"

David's cheek glowed with pleasure at the praise, and he could not refrain from telling of a brave deed performed by his father in early youth, when John Aspinall had been the means of saving a girl from an infuriated bull.

Both the gentlemen listened with much interest, and Manners quoted something from Goldsmith about a "bold peasantry, their country's pride," which raised David's spirits still higher. The conversation then took another turn, the subject was that of shooting, and the hunters were glad to find that their young comrade knew very well how to handle a musket or rifle.

"Almost the best shot that ever I met with was our gamekeeper's son," observed Manners: "I've seen him bring down a small bird on the wing when it looked a mere speck in the sky! he was such a clever lad too, he could turn his hand to anything.

He'd have been invaluable on an expedition like ours—he'd have dressed a dinner or mended a shaft, or have made a pair of moccasins, or have driven a span of oxen, as if he'd been brought up to the business of cook, carpenter, cobbler, and driver! The poor fellow was wild to come with me to Africa!"

"And why didn't you bring him?" asked Carlton.

"Well," began Manners slowly, as if he scarcely dared to give his reasons; "you see—he had got into a scrape—had been before the magistrate, and had seen the inside of a prison. I don't choose to have anyone about me whose character bears a stain."

"Quite right,—don't you think so?" said Carlton, turning towards David. The poor youth's face flushed again, but not this time with pleasure. He felt uneasy, mortified, ashamed, and knew not what to reply.

"Why," continued Carlton, seeing that he hesitated, "you would not keep company with a jailbird, would you?" Again there was a struggle within, a dialogue between the Tempter and Conscience, only carried on far more rapidly than I can write, or the reader can peruse it.

TEMPTER.—Put a bold face on the matter; say "no" at once.

CONSCIENCE.—That would be a lie.

TEMPTER.—Only a white lie; it will do no one harm.

CONSCIENCE.—It will do you grievous harm, for it is sin. *"Lying lips are an abomination to tire Lord."*

Once more David felt Conscience to represent his God's guiding eye.

"You would not keep company with a jailbird?" repeated Carlton, resolved to have a reply.

"I—I have been in a scrape myself," said David with a desperate effort.

"Then I'll be bound it was on some false charge!" exclaimed Manners.

"I wish I could say so," murmured poor David, heartily wishing himself fifty miles off.

There was silence for two or three seconds, and then Manners observed to Carlton, "whatever he was *then*, he is a noble fellow *now*; we'll never come on this subject again."

The effort was over—the truth had been told, and David had the comfort of finding that his candor had raised him as much in the favor of his friends, as he had feared that his confession would have lowered him. Manners and Carlton treated him with even more kindness than before, while he had the comfort of feeling that he had followed the dictates of Conscience, and spoken the truth, as a Christian should ever do. Never yet had any being cause to regret having followed, whether in small things or in great, the gentle leading of Him who guideth His saints by His eye!

CHAPTER NINE

THE STUBBORN SINNER

"Be ye not as the horse, or as the mute. which have no understanding: whose mouth must be held in with bit and bridle, lest they come near unto thee."—Psalm 32:9

DAVID was reminded of the verse above while watching the struggles of one of the draught-oxen, which was young, obstinate, and not yet well broken-in for the yoke. Restive and stubborn, it seemed disposed to pull in any way but the right one, though its very life, as David knew, depended on its obeying the driver, who was directing it to the nearest point where a large fountain of water was to be found. The ox kicked, tried to gore with its horns,—to break from the wagon, to do anything rather than obey, and drew down upon a itself heavy blow after heavy blow—punishment carried to an extent that would have been cruel, had it not been actually needful.

"My conduct was once very much like that of this wretched ox," thought David, "though I could a not plead its excuse of having *no understanding*. I have had terrible blows that have made my very heart bleed; but it was long before I would give way and bow my proud spirit to the yoke. But I will call it a yoke no longer; those who obey Conscience are released from *the bit and the bridle*; they follow the steps of their Master; they are not driven, but led."

The sun was sloping towards the west; and the Hottentot drivers said that the wagons would reach Quagga Fountain before he set. It was there that they would camp for the night.

"We shall not be alone," observed Carlton, "for I see a wagon not half a mile ahead."

This was rather a subject of surprise, as David was certain that none had passed on the tract since Hans Kuhe had gone that way.

"It must be that of the Boer," he observed, "but still it is strange to see it there. He counted upon leaving Quagga Fountain early this morning, A and it that be his wagon yonder, he can never have reached the water at all."

"Perhaps," suggested Manners, "his oxen were too feeble to draw the wagon, and so he has stopped, and taken the weary beasts to the fountain, leaving the wagon until they were able to pull it again."

"We shall soon know the truth," said Carlton.

"I hope the Boer may be there; that he has stuck fast in the sand: and that David may have the pleasure of giving back the purse himself, and seeing if it be possible to make such a fellow blush."

After the wagons had advanced some way David spoke again, anxiously. "Certainly there are none of the oxen with the wagon, and, strange to say, there does not seem to be anyone left in charge. Hans Kuhe is not the man to desert his goods like that."

"Though he could desert his faithful servant," observed Carlton.

"There is a man,—and it must be the Boer himself, for he is certainly not a Tottie, laying flat upon the ground, about five yards to the left of the wagon, and he looks as if he had been stripped of half his clothes!" said Manners.

"Something must have happened to him! "exclaimed David, starting up; "Hans Kuhe must have been attacked by the Bushmen. Let us hasten on and see."

The oxen were urged to their best speed. Every yard that they advanced served to confirm the fears of David. He saw before him the wagon of Kuhe, but it was utterly empty, stripped of all the innumerable articles of furniture, dress, trade, the leather garments, cooking-utensils, ivory tusks, skins, ostrich-eggs and feathers, that had made it appear something between a house on wheels, and a travelling museum. One wounded dog which came barking up to David, as if delighted to see his familiar face, was the only thing that showed life and motion. One or two arrows such as are used by Bushmen, a biscuit-box robbed of its contents, and some broken pipes and empty bottles lay on the sand, which had evidently been trampled by many feet that had never worn shoes.

The first care of the three Englishmen was to hasten up to what had appeared to be the lifeless body of the Boer. David, in his eagerness, sprang down from the wagon, nearly forgetting his lameness.

"He is not dead!" exclaimed the youth, "he is not dead! See—he moves—he opens his eyes. If we had water—"

"Brandy—brandy!" groaned the Boer. Both water and brandy were brought. The wretched man, who had lain there for twenty-four hours, drank as if he never would cease from drinking.

"He's not much hurt, I hope!" cried David; "that wound from the dart in his shoulder may not be deep; it has scarcely bled at all, and it is near no vital part."

"But the flesh is dreadfully swollen around it," said Manners, gravely shaking his head. He then quickly returned to his own wagon, to bring from it other that might be needed by the wounded man.

"How came you here!" exclaimed Hans Kuhe suddenly, fixing his eyes with a wild startled expression upon David, who had been supporting the Boer's head on his knee, while holding a flask to his lips.

"You may well ask that question," muttered Carlton, "for it is no thanks to you that he is here, or anywhere on this earth!"

He probably did not intend that his words should reach the Dutchman's ear, but they had been both heard and understood, for Hans exclaimed with vehemence, raising himself with an effort to a sitting posture as he spoke, "Ay, ay, it was that which has brought the ruin upon me! He would have watched, have kept awake; the savages would not have stolen upon us, and struck before I could snatch up a musket! Ay, ay, I've had nothing but ill-luck since I left him alone! First I dropped my purse..."

"Which David found—and which David restores to you!" said Manners, who came up at the moment, as he drew forth the purse, and gave it to the youth, who was still on his knees beside his former master.

"Take it—all your money is there, save the one piece which you owed me," said David, putting the heavy purse close to the coarse brown fingers that were wont to clutch gold so eagerly, and to hold it so fast. But, to his surprise, Hans Kuhe made no attempt to take up the purse.

"What's money to me!" groaned the miserable man, sinking back on the sand; "can it keep back death for one hour—one moment?"

"Not death!" exclaimed David, cheeringly; "you have but a flesh-wound from an arrow."

"But the arrow was *poisoned!*" muttered Hans; "there's nothing on earth that can save me!"

"He speaks too truly," said Manners, who had been examining the wound; "spend what time is left you, unhappy man, in making your peace with God, for no human skill can help you now."

"Peace with God!" repeated the sufferer gloomily; "it is too late. I never cared for religion in health, and now—"

"Pray, oh! pray I" exclaimed David. "God is so merciful—I have found Him so merciful,—if we but repent."

"I cannot repent," groaned the dying sinner, whose life had been one long course of rebellion, who had closed his ears and his heart to offers of mercy, till he had become stubborn and hardened in guilt.

"Let me but repeat to you what has been my own comfort—my own hope," said David with emotion, for Conscience bade him make yet one effort more for the soul of the miserable man,— though the presence of the hunters, and his own consciousness of unworthiness, made it very difficult for him to speak; "*Blessed is he whose—*"

"There's no blessing for me—none!" interrupted the Boer; "go, boy, go,—you mean kindly, but it is too late! Take the purse— keep it,—I have wronged you,—I've received what is due me,— money—oxen—goods—life—all gone! I shall want nothing more—but a grave!"

These were the last words which Hans ever spoke. He was gently placed in a wagon, and there David, with such care and kindness as a son might have shown, tended his enemy while life ebbed away. How awful is the deathbed of the wicked!

David had prayed to his God *in a time when He might be found*; Hans was like those unhappy ones who neglected Noah's warnings till God's people had entered the Ark, and the door was shut, and they who had been offered mercy in vain were swept away by the flood of great waters!

It is scarcely necessary to relate how the misfortune of Hans had come upon him. After eating and drinking to excess the Boer had fallen into a heavy sleep in his wagon. Pollux, who never worked if he could possibly be idle, followed his master's example and slept, while the tired oxen halted on the way. A crouching Bushman, who had come as a spy, saw the state of affairs, which was such as to invite an attack; and gathering some of his tribe, they made an onslaught on the wagon, first sending a shower of poisoned arrows, for the Boer was known to be heavily armed, was a dead shot, and a very powerful man. The reader knows the result: Pollux fled,—the oxen and everything that could be carried off were taken, and the Boer was left to die! There he lay, thirsting, and in misery, dreading attack from wild beasts, in far more woeful state than that to which his selfish cruelty had doomed his poor young servant David.

That night the remains of Hans Kuhe were buried near the Quagga Fountain. There was not a tear shed over his grave. Sadly, his life had been without faith or repentance; and his death was without hope or peace. *There is no peace, saith my God, for the wicked.*

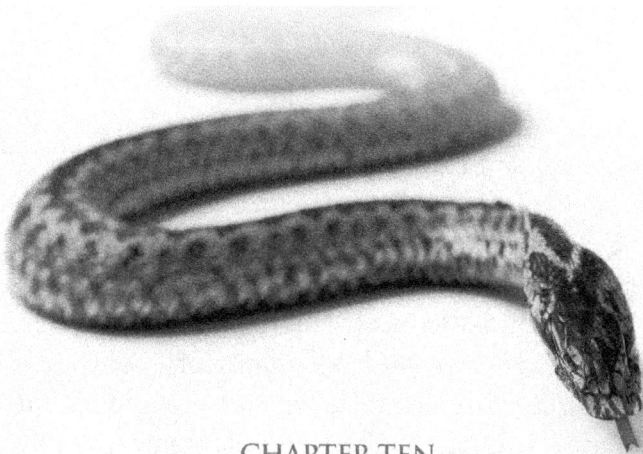

CHAPTER TEN

HOME

"Many sorrows shall be to the wicked; but he that trusteth in the Lord, mercy shall compass him about. Be glad in the Lord, and rejoice, ye righteous; and shout for joy, all ye that are upright in heart. —Psalm 32:10, 11

I WILL now pass over some months, and change the scene of my story from the wild glowing wastes of Africa, to a quiet little English farm,—and ask my reader to unfasten in thought the latch of its little gate, which is whitened with silvery frost, cross the small garden where the snow lies so thick that every footstep leaves its print, and through the low porch hung with icicles, enter the old picturesque dwelling, which feels so warm and comfortable after the sharp evening air without.

Warm it is,—for large logs are blazing in the old-fashioned fireplace, which is so wide that it holds a seat on either side; and on one of these seats is Farmer Aspinall, warming his hands by the kindly blaze, after a good day's work. His wife is stirring something in a large iron pot which is simmering on the fire, and giving out a very savory smell. Five girls of differing heights, from Minnie, a gentle-looking young maiden now almost as tall as her mother,—to Nelly who is hardly higher than the table, are busy with a quantity of bright holly and mistletoe, which Eliza had just brought in. For the scene is Christmas eve, and the farmer's family love keeping the old English custom of decorating their home with evergreens, and making it festive with berries.

"Why do you look so sad, Jenny?" asked Nelly, glancing up inquiringly into the face of her sister. "Is not this Christmas-time, and should we not all be glad?"

"Christmas has never seemed the same to me," said Jenny with a deep sigh, "since Davy went away."

"Ah! yes," cried chubby-cheeked Eliza, "how merry he used to make us all!"

"His going has been a trial,—a very great trial to us," said Minnie, to whom the events related in the second chapter had been like a blight in the springtime of life; "but our *trials* must not make us forget our *blessings*,—and we have had so many of these lately."

"Yes, there's the cow that uncle White gave us," interrupted Nelly.

"I shall never care for it as I cared for poor Crummie," said Bessy, the second youngest of the girls.

"And there's the famous harvest!" cried Eliza; "our barn was never so full before!"

"And father is better—dear father! He don't want his crutch," said Nelly.

"Oh!" exclaimed Minnie, her eyes filling up with tears, "when I look at that crutch hung up there, and think of all that father once suffered, I feel that we can never be thankful enough to see him so well again!"

"He has a sore heart though, I know he has, and so has mother," said Jenny, lowering her voice that her parents might not overhear her; "I dare say they are both thinking of poor Davy now. I'm sure since we got that last dull letter from Heinbok Kloof (what a horrid place it must be!) I've scarce thought of anything else. I wish Christmas-time were over—just think what a Christmas our Davy will have!" and a tear dropped on the spray of holly which Jenny held in her hand.

"Dear Jenny, is it not a comfort that, though parted, we can pray for him still?" said Minnie.

"I always pray for Davy," exclaimed little Nelly; "I say, 'Please, God, take care of brother, and bring him safe back.' And so," added the child with simple faith, "I think he'll come home at last."

"Listen!" cried Jenny suddenly, "isn't that a footstep outside?"

"Someone is tapping at the pane!" cried Nelly.

"There's a face at the window!" cried Minnie.

But it was the mother's eye which first caught sight of that face, and knew it in the reflected glow from the fire-light within. There was a wild rush of all the sisters to the door; but it was the mother's hand that drew back the bolt, and let in the Wanderer—the beloved; and the first kiss of welcome to David was the kiss of the mother who, sobbing, pressed him to her heart!

Yes, it was David himself, though a good deal changed, as his family saw when they were calm enough to think of anything but the one delight of meeting. He was taller, thinner, and much more sunburnt than when they had parted. But the change *within* was far greater than the change *without*; the proud, willful, wayward lad had come back the brave, unselfish, earnest Christian, who was resolved, by God's grace, to lead a new life; ever setting duty before pleasure, or rather finding his pleasure in duty: *Not slothful in business, fervent in spirit, serving the Lord.*

The farmer had started to his feet at the first joyful cry from his girls, and went forward to meet his son with such deep, quiet thankfulness as no words, no outward sign could express. The sisters were full of eager questionings, the father hardly uttered a word: the mother wept for. joy, but the father shed no tear. Yet no one could have looked at his honest manly face on that evening, as John Aspinall sat listening to the account of the wonderful deliverances of his son, without seeing that in none of the breathless listeners was feeling more true and a deep. The Christian man had gone through a life of toil, hardship, and trial; he had known sickness and suffering, poverty and disappointment; but he had put his trust in God, and God had now brought him safely through all. To Him who had been his Rock and Fortress in the time of sorrow, John Aspinall now looked up in his hour of exceeding joy.

Many sorrows shall be to the wicked. Yes, the reader may observe, but is it not also written, *Many are the afflictions of the righteous?* True, but it is added, *The Lord delivereth him out of them all.* The troubles of those who love God do not last forever, and they leave a blessing behind—like:

"*Summer showers that make the world the greener,
The air still fresher, and the sky sereener;*"

or like the overflowings of the river Nile, which cover the fields for a while, only that they may, at a future time, of the year, be covered with a more abundant harvest.

Reader, my tale is ended;—but before you lay it down, allow me to ask you a few brief questions. Do *you* know anything of the blessedness of him whose transgression is forgiven, whose sin is covered; or are you putting off repentance to a more "convenient" season, which may never arrive?

Are you one of those whom the Lord, through the voice of conscience, guides with His eye; or are you the stubborn self-seeking sinner, for whom is needed the bit, the bridle, and the blow?

Do you pray to the Lord in your troubles, or only seek help from man?

If you be willing *now* to seek the Lord *while He may be found*, to come to your Savior for pardon and peace, and the grace of His Holy Spirit, to make you love and obey Him, you will find that He is the best of masters, the truest of friends, the most tender of fathers. Walking in His ways, and doing His will, you will experience in the end the truth of the closing verses of this beautiful Psalm,— *"He that trusteth in the Lord, mercy shall compass him about. Be glad in the Lord, and rejoice, ye righteous; and shout for joy, all ye that are upright in heart."*

Psalm 32

"Blessed is he whose transgression is forgiven, whose sin is covered.

Blessed is the man unto whom the Lord imputeth not iniquity, and in whose spirit there is no guile.

When I kept silence, my bones waxed old through my roaring all the day long. For day and night Thy hand was heavy upon me: my moisture is turned into the drought of summer. Selah.

I acknowledged my sin unto Thee, and mine iniquity have I not bid. I said, I will confess my transgressions unto the Lord; and Thou forgavest the iniquity of my sin. Selah.

For this shall every one that is godly pray unto Thee in a time when Thou mayest be found: surely in the floods of great waters they shall not come nigh unto him.

Thou art my hiding-place; Thou shalt preserve me from trouble; Thou shalt compass me about with songs of deliverance. Selah.

I will instruct thee and teach thee in the way which thou shalt go: I will guide thee with mine eye.

Be ye not as the horse, or as the mule, which have no understanding; whose mouth must be held in with bit and bridle, lest they come near unto thee.

Many sorrows shall be to the wicked: but he that trusteth in the Lord, mercy shall compass him about.

Be glad in the Lord, and rejoice, ye righteous; and shout for joy, all ye that are upright in heart."

THE END

ABOUT THE AUTHOR

Charlotte Maria Tucker was an English writer, who wrote numerous popular children's didactic books that had great success in Britain and the United States. Known by the pseudonym 'A. L. O. E.,' (i.e. A Lady Of England), she was, born on May 8th, 1821, the sixth child and third daughter of Henry St. George Tucker and his wife Jane, daughter of Robert Boswell of Edinburgh, a writer to the signet. In 1822 the Tucker family settled in London where Charlotte was educated at home, and as a girl was fond of writing verses and plays. In her father's house she saw much society; among her father's friends were the Duke of Wellington, Lord Metcalfe, Lord Glenelg, and Sir Henry Pottinger.

It was not until after the death of her father in 1851 that she began her literary career. Her first book, *Claremont Tales*, was published in 1852, and from that date until her death scarcely a year passed without one or more productions from her pen. She devoted the proceeds of her books to charitable purposes.

On the death of Charlotte's mother in 1869, the London house was given up, and for the next six years Charlotte lived with her brother St. George. For some time Miss Tucker had thought of undertaking missionary work in India, and finding herself in 1875 without home ties, and with sufficient means to render her independent of missionary funds, she set off to India as an independent member of the Church of England Zenana Society. Batala, a populous city, became the centre of her missionary work. In 1878 the Baring High School for native Christian boys was permanently established at Batala, and under its shadow Miss Tucker resided, taking great interest in the pupils. At times she was the only Englishwoman within twenty miles. She helped by her liberality to found a 'plough' school for Indian boys not yet Christians, who as soon as they became converts were drafted into the high school.

Much of Miss Tucker's work consisted in writing booklets—allegories and parables—for translation into the vernacular dialects of India. Many of her books were published by the Christian Literary Society and the Punjaub Religious Book Society, and sold more widely than almost any other of their productions. At the end of 1885 Miss Tucker had a serious illness, and never fully recovered. In 1893 she fell ill again, and she died at Amritsar on Dec. 2nd, 1893. She was buried at Batala on Dec.

5th, in accordance with the terms of her will, without a coffin, at a cost not exceeding five rupees. There is an inscription to her memory in the Uran dialect in the church at Batala.

Miss Tucker was a woman of tireless energy and stern determination; but her sociable temperament endeared her to all with whom she came in contact in India, both natives and English. Her industry was unceasing. The British Museum's catalogue has 142 separate entries of books published by her between 1854 and 1893. Most of the tales are allegorical in form, with an obtrusive moral.

From Agnes Giberne's *A Lady of England; the Life and Letters of Charlotte Maria Tucker*, 1895.

THE MISSION OF GREAT CHRISTIAN BOOKS

The ministry of Great Christian Books was established to glorify The Lord Jesus Christ and to be used by Him to expand and edify the kingdom of God while we occupy and anticipate Christ's glorious return. Great Christian Books will seek to accomplish this mission by publishing Gospel literature which is biblically faithful, relevant, and practically applicable to many of the serious spiritual needs of mankind upon the beginning of this new millennium. To do so we will always seek to boldly incorporate the truths of Scripture, especially those which were largely articulated as a body of theology during the Protestant Reformation of the sixteenth century and ensuing years. We gladly join our voice in the proclamations of— Scripture Alone, Faith Alone, Grace Alone, Christ Alone, and God's Glory Alone!

Our ministry seeks the blessing of our God as we seek His face to both confirm and support our labors for Him. Our prayers for this work can be summarized by two verses from the Book of Psalms:

> "...let the beauty of the LORD our God be upon us, And establish the work of our hands for us; Yes, establish the work of our hands."—Psalm 90:17

> "Not unto us, O LORD, not unto us, but to your name give glory." —Psalm 115:1

Great Christian Books appreciates the financial support of anyone who shares our burden and vision for publishing literature which combines sound Bible doctrine and practical exhortation in an age when too few so-called "Christian" publications do the same. We thank you in advance for any assistance you can give us in our labors to fulfill this important mission. May God bless you.

For a catalog of other great
Christian books including
additional wholesome
Christian fictional works
contact us in
any of the following ways:

write us at:
Great Christian Books
160 37th Street
Lindenhurst, NY 11757

call us at:
631. 956. 0998

find us online:
www.greatchristianbooks.com

email us at:
mail@greatchristianbooks.com

www.ingramcontent.com/pod-product-compliance
Lightning Source LLC
Chambersburg PA
CBHW021204020426
42331CB00003B/196